Hi and Lois

HOW DO YOU SPELL DAD?

By Mort Walker and Dik Browne

The cartoons in this volume also appear in the Giant Size HI AND LOIS: HOME SWEAT HOME!

TOR

A Tom Doherty Associates Book

HI AND LOIS: HOW DO YOU SPELL DAD?

Copyright © 1980, 1981, 1985 by King Features Syndicate, Inc.

The cartoons in this volume also appear in the Giant Size HI AND LOIS: HOME SWEAT HOME!

First printing: October 1985

A TOR Book

Published by Tom Doherty Associates
49 West 24 Street
New York, N.Y. 10010

ISBN: 0-812-56900-8
CAN. ED.: 0-812-56901-6

Printed in the United States of America

0 9 8 7 6 5 4 3 2 1

© 1981 King Features Syndicate, Inc. World rights reserved

10-11

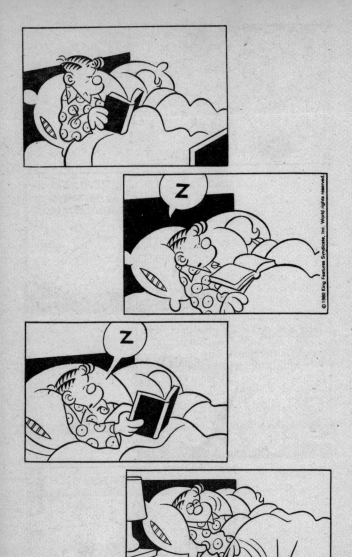

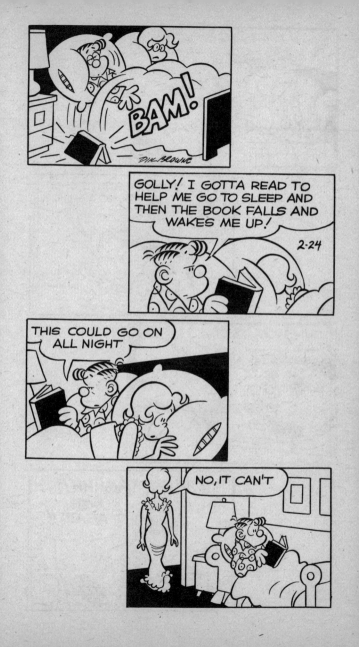

BEETLE BAILEY
THE WACKIEST G.I. IN THE ARMY